THIS COOKBOOK BELONGS TO:

_____

BLUEBERRIES
FOR SAL
COOKBOOK

BLUEBERRIES FOR SAL COOKBOOK

Sweet Recipes Inspired by
the Beloved Children's Classic

ROBERT McCLOSKEY

Additional Illustrations by Piers Sanford

Clarkson Potter/Publishers
New York

Contents

Introduction 6

Introduction

BLUEBERRIES FOR SAL WAS ORIGINALLY PUBLISHED in 1948, the fourth book of the eight that Robert McCloskey would eventually write. It tells the story of Little Sal and her mother as they went about picking blueberries on Blueberry Hill, as well as Little Bear and his mother who were out eating berries on the same summer day.

McCloskey fell in love with Maine in the summer of 1946, when he visited for the first time. He and his wife bought a home on an island off the coast of Maine before the end of that same summer. In *Blueberries for Sal* and so many of his other books, McCloskey's art captured the homespun elegance of Maine, his beloved home, and made it real for hundreds of thousands of readers around the world. The characters of Little Sal and her mother are based on Robert McCloskey's own Little Sal, his daughter Sally, and his wife, Peggy. A simple story accompanied by dark blue illustrations, it became a Caldecott Honoree and a beloved classic. Since then, it has touched generations of adults and children who love the *kuplink, kuplank, kuplunk* of little berries in a mostly empty pail. In 2000 McCloskey was named a Living Legend by the U.S. Library of Congress, an honor he enjoyed for several years before his death in 2003.

We know Little Sal and her mother started canning their harvest once they got home, but there the story ends. This book can give you lots of sweeter ways to enjoy your own blueberries whenever you wish. Sip on a Berry Blue Smoothie or maybe enjoy a slice of Blueberry Upside-Down Cake as an afternoon snack. Bring a tray of Blueberry Maple Pecan Scones to share with friends or bake a batch of Moose Track Blondies for dessert. The recipes are simple and many of the steps are easy for little hands if you have helpers in the kitchen. Most of them work just as well with frozen berries as they do with fresh, and on a few occasions frozen is noted as the best option for the recipe. So no matter what time of year, you can enjoy these treats with the people you love.

Sprinkled throughout the recipes are illustrations from *Blueberries for Sal* alongside new illustrations inspired by McCloskey's distinctive art style. You'll also find information about blueberries, about *Blueberries for Sal,* and about Robert McCloskey's legacy.

Sal and her mother bring their blueberries home to enjoy all winter long. Whether you spend your summers picking berries or just want to bake up a sweet treat with fruit from the freezer, you can enjoy those blueberries all year long, too.

Blueberry Jam

makes 1 pint

5 cups (about 1½ pounds) fresh
   or frozen blueberries

¾ cup sugar

¼ cup fresh lemon juice

⅓ teaspoon kosher salt

1. Add the blueberries, sugar, 3 tablespoons of the lemon juice, and the salt to a medium saucepan and stir to coat. Turn the heat on to medium and cook, stirring often, until the mixture gets very juicy and starts to bubble, 4 to 8 minutes (depending on whether you're using fresh or frozen berries and how large the berries are).

2. Once the mixture is bubbling at a good rate, reduce the heat to medium-low so it is at a gentle simmer and cook, stirring occasionally, until you can tilt the pan and drag a wooden spoon across the bottom and it leaves a trail that doesn't fill in immediately, about 30 minutes (the mixture will still look quite thin).

3. Turn off the heat and set aside to cool, stirring occasionally, for about 30 minutes, then add the remaining 1 tablespoon of lemon juice and transfer to a clean pint-size jar. Leave uncovered at room temperature until completely cool, then cover and refrigerate for at least 2 hours before serving. The jam will thicken as it chills. It can be stored in the fridge for up to 2 weeks.

Blueberry Lemonade

Makes 5 cups

1 cup sugar
1 cup fresh or frozen blueberries
1 cup fresh lemon juice (from 7 to
   8 lemons)
Ice
1 lemon sliced
   into wheels

1. Heat the sugar and 1 cup of water in a medium saucepan over medium heat, stirring occasionally, until the sugar dissolves, 2 to 3 minutes. Add the blueberries and simmer, stirring occasionally, until they burst, 2 to 3 minutes. Turn off the heat and set aside to cool to room temperature.

2. Strain the mixture through a fine-mesh sieve and into an airtight container, using a silicone spatula to push down on the solids to get as much liquid as possible out of them (discard the blueberry solids). Refrigerate until completely chilled, at least 2 hours or up to 1 week.

3. Pour the blueberry syrup into a large pitcher. Add 2½ cups of cold water and the lemon juice and serve over ice with a lemon wheel in the glass.

BEARS ARE OMNIVORES, BUT when it comes to bears of North America, their diet is largely vegetarian and they eat lots and lots of berries. Blueberries, of course, but they'll also spend the summer eating strawberries, raspberries, chokecherries—basically any small, soft fruits they can get their paws on. Just like Little Bear and his mom, bears will spend many hours of the day eating berries in order to store up calories for their winter hibernation.

There are several kinds of bears native to North America--the grizzly bear (sometimes called a brown bear), the black bear, and the polar bear. But only one kind of bear lives in Maine--the black bear. If you've ever wondered what kind of bear Little Bear is, now you can know for sure.

BLUEBERRIES ARE ONE OF THE few fruits native to North America. The small wild varieties thrived on the continent for hundreds, probably thousands, of years before they were cultivated and shipped around the world. The plants were first successfully cultivated in 1912, and the first commercial crop was sold in 1916. Those are the berries you're most likely to see in the grocery store.

There are four types of blueberries: highbush, lowbush, hybrid half-high, and rabbiteye. The most commonly planted blueberry, and the one you're most likely to see in stores, is the highbush. The small blueberry known as "wild," and the one that Little Sal and her mother picked on Blueberry Hill, is the lowbush blueberry.

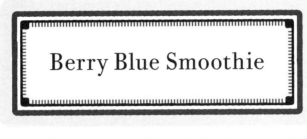

Berry Blue Smoothie

Makes 2 smoothies (about 3½ cups)

1 medium banana, peeled
1½ cups frozen blueberries
¼ cup rolled oats
4 dried apricots or pitted dates
1½ cups dairy or nondairy milk
2 to 4 tablespoons honey or agave syrup

1. Add the banana, blueberries, oats, apricots, milk, and 2 tablespoons honey to the jar of a blender. Cover and blend on high speed until smooth.

2. Divide into 2 tall glasses, taste and add more sweetener if needed, and serve with straws.

Blueberry Overnight Oats

<u>*Serves* 4</u>

¾ cup steel-cut oats

¾ teaspoon kosher salt

½ cup dried blueberries

Milk or nondairy milk

Maple syrup or Blueberry-Maple
  Syrup (page 27), for serving

1. Add 3 cups of water, the oats, and the salt to
   a medium saucepan and bring to a strong boil
   over medium-high heat. Reduce the heat to
   medium or medium-low and simmer gently for
   2 minutes.

2. Turn off the heat, stir in the dried blueberries, cover the saucepan, and set aside for 30 minutes.

3. Transfer the oats to an airtight container and refrigerate overnight.

4. In the morning, warm the oats in a microwave or in a saucepan with enough milk to create the consistency you prefer (see Note). Divide among four bowls and serve with a drizzle of syrup.

~~~~~~~~ NOTE ~~~~~~~~

Instead of rewarming the oats with milk, you can scoop the cold oats into a bowl and top with a scoop of your favorite yogurt and a handful of fresh blueberries.

BLUEBERRIES AREN'T JUST DELICIOUS, they're also a superfood. They're believed to have some of the highest levels of antioxidants of all common fruits and vegetables. Those antioxidants are said to help neutralize free radicals that can damage your DNA, which in turn could help protect against some cancers, as well as the negative effects of aging. Blueberries are also high in manganese and vitamins C and K, and provide a surprising amount of fiber for such a small berry. Some studies have indicated that they can also help lower blood pressure and cholesterol and reduce the risk of heart disease. So eat as many as you'd like—they're good for you!

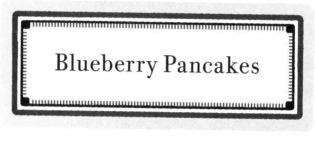

Blueberry Pancakes

Makes 10 pancakes

1¾ cups all-purpose flour

1½ teaspoons baking powder

½ teaspoon baking soda

1 teaspoon kosher salt

1¼ cups buttermilk

2 tablespoons canola oil

1 teaspoon vanilla extract

2 large eggs

3 tablespoons sugar

1 to 1½ cups fresh or frozen
   blueberries (depending on how
   large your berries are)

Nonstick cooking spray

6 tablespoons unsalted butter, melted

Warmed maple syrup or Blueberry-Maple Syrup (recipe follows), for serving

1. In a medium bowl, whisk together the flour, baking powder, baking soda, and salt.

2. In a 2-cup liquid measure, whisk together the buttermilk, oil, and vanilla.

3. In a large bowl, use a whisk or hand mixer to beat the eggs and sugar until thick and creamy, 1 to 2 minutes. Whisk in the buttermilk mixture, then whisk in the flour mixture until no traces of flour remain. Stir in the blueberries.

4. Heat a griddle or large nonstick pan over medium heat. Coat the surface with cooking

Recipe continues

spray and add a heaping ¼ cup of batter to the pan for each pancake. Once there are bubbles across the surfaces of the pancakes, the edges begin to look dry, and the bottoms are golden brown, 1 to 2 minutes, use a spatula to flip the pancakes over (you may need to fiddle with the heat, lowering or increasing it as necessary). Cook on the other side until browned and the center of the pancakes resist light pressure, 1 to 2 minutes longer. Spoon melted butter over each pancake and transfer to plates or a platter and continue with the remaining batter.

5. Serve the pancakes with warmed syrup.

NOTE

To make the pancakes dairy-free, use nondairy unsweetened milk with 1 tablespoon of lemon or lime juice whisked in for the buttermilk, and nondairy butter in place of cow's milk butter. To make them egg-free, substitute ⅓ cup of applesauce for the eggs and add another ½ teaspoon baking powder to the flour mixture.

BLUEBERRY-MAPLE SYRUP

To a small saucepan add ½ cup maple syrup and
½ cup of blueberries and warm over medium
heat until the berries soften and burst. Serve over
pancakes, ice cream, or Greek-style yogurt. You can
also strain out the blueberries for a smooth syrup if
you prefer.

Blueberry Muffins

Makes 12 muffins

Nonstick cooking spray

1 lemon

1 cup sugar

½ cup dairy or nondairy
   (unsweetened) milk

1½ teaspoons vanilla extract

2 cups all-purpose flour

1½ teaspoons baking powder

¼ teaspoon baking soda

1 teaspoon kosher salt

1 stick (8 tablespoons) unsalted
   butter, at room temperature

2 large eggs

1¾ cups fresh or frozen
   blueberries

1. Preheat the oven to 375°F. Line a 12-cup muffin tin with muffin liners. Spray the liners and tin with cooking spray and set aside.

2. Use a rasp grater to zest the lemon into a medium bowl. Add the sugar and rub the sugar and zest together until it's very fragrant and looks wet like sand. Scoop out 3 tablespoons and set aside in a small dish (this will be for making the sparkly muffin tops).

3. Halve the lemon and squeeze the lemon juice into a 1-cup liquid measure. Add the milk and vanilla and set aside (the lemon juice will curdle the milk—this is good!).

4. In a separate medium bowl, whisk together the flour, baking powder, baking soda, and salt.

 Recipe continues

5. Add the soft butter to the large amount of lemon sugar and cream together using a hand mixer or wooden spoon. Add one of the eggs and beat to combine until airy, 10 to 15 seconds. Add the other egg and do the same.

6. Add a third of the flour mixture to the egg mixture and mix in until there are just a few dry spots. Mix in half the liquid and beat for

10 seconds to lighten. Add half the remaining flour and repeat with the remaining liquid, beating to lighten.

7. Add the blueberries to the remaining flour in the bowl, then add both the blueberries and flour to the batter and gently stir until combined (don't overstir or the blueberries will turn the batter blue). Use a large spoon or scoop to divide the batter among the muffin cups and then top each muffin with the reserved lemon sugar.

8. Bake until the muffins are golden brown and the centers resist light pressure, 28 to 32 minutes. Remove from the oven and set aside to cool at least 20 minutes before serving. Store in an airtight container for up to 2 days, or wrap each muffin in plastic and freeze in a resealable zip-top bag for up to 1 month.

THIS BOOK IS FULL OF SWEET recipes for blueberries, but that doesn't mean the blueberries aren't equally delicious in savory preparations. Here are a few ideas to get you started.

- Build a fresh salad with quinoa, diced medjool dates and apples, mint, parsley, scallions, sliced carrots and bell peppers, and fresh or dried blueberries. Dress it with a balsamic or lemon vinaigrette or one made with blueberry vinegar (see page 59).

- Spoon blueberry sauce over roasted pork for a summery variation on the traditional pork chops and applesauce. Add a little balsamic vinegar to the sauce before serving to give it some tang, or keep it sweet and simple.

- Add a thick layer of blueberry jam to a grilled cheese sandwich, and throw in a few basil leaves as well. Mozzarella is a great melting cheese to pair with blueberries.

- Make a salad of watermelon, feta, and mint and throw in a cup of blueberries for color and flavor. It's a delicious side dish for any barbecue.

Blueberry Maple Pecan Scones

makes 8 scones

2¼ cups all-purpose flour,
   plus extra for shaping
¼ cup granulated sugar
2 teaspoons baking powder
1 teaspoon plus a pinch of kosher salt
6 tablespoons unsalted butter,
   cut into ½-inch pieces
1 to 1¼ cups frozen blueberries
½ cup roughly chopped pecans
¾ cup heavy cream
½ cup maple syrup
3 to 4 tablespoons confectioners'
   sugar

1. Line a rimmed sheet pan with parchment paper or a nonstick baking mat.

2. In a large bowl, whisk together the flour, granulated sugar, baking powder, and 1 teaspoon of salt.

3. Add the butter pieces to the dry ingredients and use your fingers or a pastry cutter to cut the butter into the flour until there aren't any pieces larger than a small pea. Add the blueberries and pecans and toss with your fingers. Pour in the cream and use a wooden spoon to combine, trying your best to not break up the blueberries, but also creating a dough that holds together (there shouldn't be any dry spots in the bottom of the bowl). Gather the dough into a rough ball.

4. Set the dough on top of the parchment-lined pan. Using lightly floured hands, pat the dough into a ¾-inch-thick circle. Use a knife or bench knife to cut the circle into 8 wedges, like a pie. Place the pan in the freezer and chill for 15 minutes, or refrigerate for 30 minutes.

Recipe continues

5. Preheat the oven to 425°F. Bake until the scones are golden brown and the centers resist light pressure, 12 to 15 minutes. Remove from the oven and cool on the pan 5 minutes before transferring the scones to a wire rack.

6. Immediately whisk the maple syrup, confectioners' sugar, and a pinch of salt together in a small bowl. Use a spoon to drizzle as much glaze as you like over each scone. The scones are best served warm but can be stored in an airtight container at room temperature for 1 day.

Blueberry-Almond Bear Claws

Makes 4 pastries

PASTRY

    3½ ounces (½ tube) almond paste

    ¼ cup granulated sugar

    1 large egg, separated

    One 8-ounce tube crescent roll dough

    ¼ cup homemade (page 10) or
        store-bought blueberry jam

    Pinch of kosher salt

    ⅓ cup sliced almonds

ICING

    ⅔ cup confectioners' sugar

    1 tablespoon milk

Recipe continues

1. Preheat the oven to 375° F. Line a rimmed sheet pan with parchment paper or a nonstick baking mat.

2. Make the pastry: Set a box grater over a medium bowl and grate the almond paste over the medium-hole side. Add the granulated sugar and use your fingers to crumble them together. Add the egg white and whisk until creamy (it won't be smooth).

3. Follow the package instructions to open the tube of crescent roll dough. Carefully unroll the dough onto the prepared pan. It will be perforated into 8 triangles—rather than separating the dough into individual triangles, separate it into 4 rectangles (each being made of 2 triangles). Press the perforations slightly to close the seam.

4. Divide the almond paste mixture among the centers of the dough rectangles (about a generous 1 tablespoon each). Top with 1 tablespoon of blueberry jam. Fold the long side over to meet the edge of the other long side and press all the way around to seal. Use

a knife to cut three ½- to ¾-inch slits at the bottom edge of each pastry (as the pastry bakes, these will become the claws—don't slice too deeply otherwise the filling may leak out a little while baking).

5. Add the egg yolk to a small bowl and whisk with 1 tablespoon of water and the salt. Brush the egg wash over each pastry, then sprinkle with the sliced almonds, pressing down slightly on the almonds to adhere.

6. Bake until the pastry and almonds are golden brown, 18 to 20 minutes. Remove from the oven and set aside to cool.

7. While the pastry cools, make the icing: In a small bowl, whisk together the confectioners' sugar and milk until smooth. Drizzle the icing over the cooled bear claws and let it set for 5 minutes before eating. The bear claws can be kept at room temperature for 2 days and are best slightly warmed before serving.

JULY IS NATIONAL BLUEBERRY Month in the U.S., a decision that ties back to the fruit's cultivation history. The first commercial crop of blueberries was developed in 1916 in New Jersey, and that particular plant had a growing season that made the berries ready to eat in July. Then in 1974, President Richard Nixon first recognized July as National Blueberry Month. But it wasn't until 2003 that the U.S. Department of Agriculture officially recognized National Blueberry Month as a recurring event to celebrate.

Blueberries are also recognized on a smaller scale by several states. The wild blueberry became Maine's state berry in 1991, and the cultivated berry was recognized as New Jersey's state berry in 2003.

Blueberry Streusel Coffee Cake

Makes <u>one 9-inch square</u> cake

Nonstick cooking spray

¾ cup plus ⅔ cup granulated sugar

1½ cups plus ⅔ cup all-purpose flour

¼ cup packed light or dark brown sugar

2 teaspoons ground cinnamon

1 stick (8 tablespoons) unsalted butter, at room temperature, plus 2 tablespoons cold butter

1 cup chopped pecans or walnuts

Few pinches of flaky sea salt (optional)

2 large eggs

1 cup sour cream

2 teaspoons vanilla extract

2 teaspoons baking powder

½ teaspoon baking soda

1 teaspoon kosher salt

1½ cups fresh or frozen
   blueberries

1. Preheat the oven to 350°F. Spray a 9-inch
   square metal baking pan with cooking spray.
   You can also line the pan with two crisscrossed
   sheets of aluminum foil, leaving some overhang,
   so you can remove the entire cake from the
   pan before serving. Lightly spray the foil with
   cooking spray.

2. In a medium bowl, add the ⅔ cup of granulated
   sugar, the ⅔ cup of flour, the brown sugar, and
   cinnamon and whisk to combine. Scoop out
   and remove ¾ cup of the mixture to a second

Recipe continues

medium bowl. To the second bowl, add the 2 tablespoons cold butter and use your fingers to work the butter into the mixture. Stir in the nuts and flaky sea salt, if using, and set aside (this is the topping).

3. In a large bowl or in the bowl of a stand mixer fitted with the paddle attachment, add the remaining 8 tablespoons of softened butter and the remaining ¾ cup of granulated sugar and mix on medium-low speed until combined. Add the eggs, sour cream, and vanilla and mix on medium speed until combined (the mixture may look broken—this is okay).

4. In a medium bowl, whisk together the remaining 1½ cups of flour, the baking powder, baking soda, and salt and add to the batter. Mix on medium-low speed until combined, then increase the speed to medium-high and beat until airy, about 1 minute.

5. Use a silicone spatula to scrape half of the batter into the prepared baking pan. Sprinkle evenly with the sugar-flour mixture (the one

without the nuts and butter) and top with the blueberries. Cover with the remaining batter, smoothing out the top. Scatter with the nut-and-butter streusel topping.

6. Bake until the cake is browned on top and a toothpick inserted into the center comes out clean (if you get a streak of blueberry, test in another spot), 45 to 55 minutes. Remove from the oven and cool completely before slicing into 9 squares (3 rows by 3 columns). Store in an airtight container for up to 1 week.

Blueberry-Banana Bread

Makes <u>one</u> 8½ × 4½-inch loaf

Nonstick cooking spray

2 cups all-purpose flour

1 teaspoon baking powder

1½ teaspoons kosher salt

½ cup granulated sugar

Zest of 1 lemon

½ cup packed light brown sugar

2 large eggs

3 ripe bananas, peeled and mashed

⅓ cup sour cream

6 tablespoons unsalted butter,
   melted

1 teaspoon vanilla extract

1¼ cups fresh or frozen
    blueberries

1. Preheat the oven to 350°F. Lightly coat an
    8½ × 4½-inch loaf pan with cooking spray (or
    line the pan with aluminum foil, leaving some
    overhang, and lightly coat the foil with spray if
    you want to easily remove the loaf from the pan
    before slicing).

2. In a medium bowl, whisk together the flour,
    baking powder, and salt.

3. In the bowl of a stand mixer fitted with the
    paddle attachment, or in a large bowl if using
    a hand mixer, add the granulated sugar and
    lemon zest and use your fingers to rub the zest
    into the sugar until it is fragrant and sandy.
    Add the brown sugar and eggs and beat on
    medium-low until moistened, then increase
    the speed to medium-high and beat until well
    combined, 30 seconds to 1 minute.

 *Recipe continues*

4. Add the bananas, sour cream, melted butter, and vanilla and beat on medium until combined, about 30 seconds, scraping down the bowl as needed. Add the flour mixture and mix on low until moistened, then increase the speed to medium and beat until well combined, about 30 seconds. Remove the bowl from the mixer and use a silicone spatula to fold the blueberries in by hand.

5. Scrape the batter into the prepared pan, smoothing the top and getting into every corner, and set in the oven to bake for 15 minutes. Reduce the oven temperature to 325°F and continue to bake until the loaf is golden brown, a toothpick inserted into the center comes out clean (aside from a potential streak of blueberry!), and the center resists light pressure, 55 minutes to 1 hour and 5 minutes.

6. Remove from the oven and cool completely before slicing and serving.

W

HICH OF THESE ARE real blueberry variety names?

- Berkeley
- Blue Ribbon
- Bluecrop
- Blueray
- Brightwell
- Chickadee
- Coville
- Emerald
- Herbert
- Ivanhoe
- Jersey
- Liberty
- Meader

- Miss Jackie
- Pink Champagne
- Pink Lemonade
- Pioneer
- Powder Blue
- Springhigh
- Stanley
- Star
- Sunshine Blue
- Top Hat
- Wareham
- Windsor
- Woodard

Answer: They all are.

Blueberry Skillet Cornbread

Makes one 12-inch skillet

1 stick (8 tablespoons) unsalted
  butter
3 cups all-purpose flour
1 cup fine yellow cornmeal
1 cup sugar
2 tablespoons baking powder
1 tablespoon kosher salt
2¼ cups milk
3 large eggs
1 cup fresh or frozen blueberries

1. Preheat the oven to 350°F.

2. Add the butter to a 12-inch oven-safe skillet (cast iron is ideal!) and place the pan in the oven until the butter is melted, 5 to 10 minutes.

3. Meanwhile, in a large bowl, whisk together the flour, cornmeal, sugar, baking powder, and salt. In a medium bowl, whisk together the milk and eggs.

4. Once the butter is melted, remove the skillet from the oven and carefully swirl to coat the sides of the pan (or use a silicone basting brush). Pour the melted butter into the milk mixture, and return the now-empty buttered pan to the oven.

5. Pour the liquid ingredients over the dry ingredients and use a wooden spoon to combine them until there are no dry spots in the batter. Fold in the blueberries.

 *Recipe continues*

6. Carefully remove the skillet from the oven and use a silicone spatula to transfer the batter to the greased pan, smoothing it out into an even layer (the batter will hiss and sizzle a bit—this is good!). Place the skillet in the oven and bake until the cornbread is golden brown and the center resists light pressure, 35 to 45 minutes.

7. Remove from the oven and cool slightly before slicing and serving. Store the cornbread at room temperature for up to 3 days.

Blueberry-Oat Cookies

makes about 18 cookies

1½ cups all-purpose flour

1 cup rolled oats

1 teaspoon kosher salt

¾ teaspoon ground cinnamon

½ teaspoon baking powder

1½ sticks (12 tablespoons) unsalted
butter, at room temperature

1 cup sugar

1 large egg

¼ teaspoon almond extract or
1 teaspoon vanilla extract

¾ cup dried or dehydrated
blueberries

 Recipe continues

1. Preheat the oven to 350°F. Line a sheet pan with parchment or a nonstick baking mat and set aside. In a large bowl, whisk together the flour, oats, salt, cinnamon, and baking powder.

2. In the bowl of a stand mixer fitted with the paddle attachment, or in a large bowl if using a hand mixer, cream the butter and sugar on low speed until mixed, about 30 seconds, then increase the speed to medium-high and beat until creamy and airy, 1½ to 2 minutes.

3. Reduce the mixer speed to low, add the egg and almond extract, and beat on medium-high speed until well combined, 15 to 20 seconds or so.

4. Stop the mixer, add the dry ingredients, and mix on medium-low speed until almost combined, then add the blueberries and increase the speed to medium until the dough is well combined and no dry spots remain.

5. Shape the dough into 18 balls and set them on the prepared sheet pan in a 3 by 3 configuration so there's enough room between them to spread. Bake until the cookies are golden

around the edges and they feel baked in the center when lightly pressed, 15 to 17 minutes. Remove from the oven and cool 5 minutes on the sheet pan, then transfer to a wire rack to cool completely.

6. You can continue to bake the cookies in batches, or place the remaining dough balls in a zip-top freezer bag and freeze for up to 3 months. To bake from frozen, just add a few minutes to the baking time.

L ITTLE SAL AND HER MOTHER collected their blueberries so they could enjoy them all winter, long after blueberry season had ended. While nowadays it's easy to buy blueberries any time of year, it's also relatively easy to preserve them if you happen to go blueberry picking and end up with more than you can use.

BLUEBERRIES FREEZE WELL. Simply spread them on a sheet pan and freeze until solid, then store in a container and scoop out as needed.

YOU CAN MAKE A JAM, JELLY, OR SYRUP. Most recipes are a combination of fruit, sugar, lemon juice or citric acid, and water—less to make jam and more to make a syrup. When it's finished, you can preserve it using simple water-bath canning methods, provided you add enough lemon juice or other acid to the product you're canning.

DRIED BLUEBERRIES MAKE A CHEWY AND SWEET SNACK. If you have a dehydrator, or an oven set to its lowest possible temperature, you can easily preserve your blueberries as a shelf-stable snack. They're delicious to eat out of hand or sprinkle on dishes.

TRY MAKING BLUEBERRY VINEGAR. Simply add a handful of blueberries to plain white distilled vinegar or apple cider vinegar, simmer for five to ten minutes, and then let steep until completely cooled. The fruity, tart vinegar makes a summery vinaigrette for salads all year long.

Peanut Butter Thumbprint Cookies

makes 16 cookies

¾ cup roasted and salted peanuts

1⅓ cups packed light brown sugar

1 large egg

1½ teaspoons kosher salt

½ teaspoon vanilla extract

1 cup chunky or smooth peanut
butter (see Notes)

¼ cup homemade (page 10) or
store-bought blueberry jam

1. Line a sheet pan with parchment paper or a nonstick baking mat. Finely chop the peanuts so there are some small bits and some semismall ones and add them to a medium bowl.

2. To a large bowl or the bowl of a stand mixer, add the sugar, egg, salt, vanilla, and peanut butter. Using a hand mixer, a stand mixer fitted with the paddle attachment, or a rubber spatula, blend the mixture until well combined.

3. Shape the cookie dough into 16 balls and roll each through the peanuts, then space them on the prepared pan into 4 rows with 4 cookies each. Use your finger (or a small person's thumb) to gently press an indentation into the center of each. Freeze for 15 minutes, or refrigerate for 30 minutes or overnight (see Notes).

4. Preheat the oven to 350°F. Remove the pan from the freezer or fridge and add a heaping ½ teaspoon of blueberry jam to the center of each cookie (add a little more if you made deep indentations). Bake 5 minutes and reduce the

Recipe continues

oven temperature to 325°F. Continue to bake until golden and firm, but not hard (you might even think they could use 2 extra minutes in the oven), about 20 minutes. Remove from the oven and cool completely on the sheet pan. Store the cookies in an airtight container at room temperature for up to 5 days.

~~~~ NOTES ~~~~

If possible, avoid using all-natural peanut butter (with oil that separates from the solids), as the cookies will spread more during baking.

You can also freeze the indented dough balls on a large plate or pan until very firm, then transfer to a zip-top freezer bag and store in the freezer for up to 2 months. You will need to add a couple of minutes to the baking time.

J UST AS THEY DO IN *Blueberries for Sal*, birds love blueberries and will swoop in for a snack when they can. The most common way to protect your blueberries is by using nets. In large-scale farms, that means draping nets on top of bushes to ward off birds. If you have a home garden, it can also mean building a netted greenhouse-style structure around your bushes to fully enclose them. It's a very effective way to keep birds, like crows and partridges, out of the blueberries without causing any harm.

Moose Track Blondies

Makes 9 bars

2 sticks (16 tablespoons) unsalted
  butter, at room temperature
1 cup packed light brown sugar
1 cup granulated sugar
2 large eggs
2 teaspoons vanilla extract
2 cups all-purpose flour
2 teaspoons baking powder
1 teaspoon kosher salt
1 cup white chocolate chips
½ cup roasted and salted cashews,
  roughly chopped (optional)
1 cup frozen blueberries

Nonstick cooking spray or
    1 tablespoon unsalted butter
    at room temperature
Flaky sea salt (optional)  *Recipe continues*

1. In a large bowl with a hand mixer, or in the bowl of a stand mixer fitted with the paddle attachment, cream the butter with the brown and granulated sugars on low speed until combined. Increase the speed to medium-high and beat until pale and airy, about 3 minutes if using a hand mixer or 2 minutes if using a stand mixer.

2. Add the eggs one at a time, beating well after each addition, and adding the vanilla at the end. Use a silicone spatula to scrape down the bottom and sides of the bowl as needed.

3. In a medium bowl, whisk together the flour, baking powder, and kosher salt, then add to the butter mixture and beat on medium-low to combine. Add the chocolate chips and cashews, if using, and fold into the dough until they're mostly incorporated, then add the blueberries and continue to fold in until well combined. (But stop short of making the dough blue! A few blue streaks are unavoidable.)

4. Lightly coat a 9-inch square baking pan with the cooking spray or softened butter (you can also line the pan with aluminum foil, leaving a bit of overhang, then lightly coat the foil with spray or butter—this makes it easy if you want to remove the entire square of blondies before cutting). Add the dough to the pan, pressing it into all the corners so it is even. Refrigerate while you preheat the oven to 350°F (or refrigerate overnight and bake the next day).

5. Sprinkle with flaky salt, if using, then bake until browned and a toothpick inserted into the center comes out clean, 30 to 34 minutes. Remove from the oven and cool at least 30 minutes before slicing into 9 squares (3 rows by 3 columns). Store in the pan (or in an airtight container) at room temperature for up to 1 week.

BLUEBERRIES FOR SAL IS celebrated in other ways besides blueberry dishes. At the Coastal Maine Botanical Gardens, there's a sculpture called *Sal's Bear* of a baby bear and spilled pail of blueberries. The sculpture, created by Nancy Schön and dedicated in 2010, is based on the drawings in McCloskey's book. Schön also created the iconic *Make Way for Ducklings* sculpture in the Boston Public Garden.

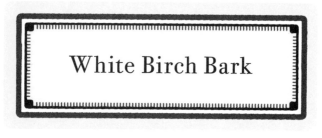

White Birch Bark

Makes about 1½ cups

¼ cup slivered almonds

¼ cup unsweetened shredded
coconut

8 ounces good-quality white
chocolate, finely chopped
(1 to 1¼ cups; don't use white
chocolate chips)

½ cup dried or dehydrated
blueberries

1. Preheat the oven to 350°F. Line a rimmed sheet pan with parchment paper and add the nuts. Bake for 4 minutes, remove from the oven, and add the coconut. Continue to bake for 4 to 5 minutes, stirring midway through, until both are lightly toasted. Remove from the oven and set aside. (Once the sheet pan is cool, carefully lift the parchment with the nuts and coconut and set aside; line the sheet pan with a fresh sheet of parchment for the bark.)

2. Add three-fourths of the chocolate to a medium heat-safe bowl. Add 1 inch of water to a medium saucepan and bring to a simmer over high heat. Reduce the heat to low and set the bowl on top (the bottom of the bowl shouldn't touch the water). Stir the chocolate every 30 seconds to 1 minute, until it is completely melted. Stir in the remaining chocolate and carefully remove the bowl from the saucepan (this chocolate will mostly melt—and some will stay in small pieces, offering a nice bark-y texture).

 Recipe continues

3. Pour the white chocolate out onto the prepared pan and use a silicone spatula to gently spread it out (not too thin—just a bit thicker than a Hershey's bar). Sprinkle the coconut, almonds, and blueberries on top and set aside until the chocolate is completely firm, about 30 minutes if your kitchen isn't too warm (you can place the pan in the refrigerator or freezer to help it along).

4. Break the bark into large pieces and place it in an airtight container for up to 1 week.

BLUEBERRIES ARE RELATED to cranberries, bilberries, huckleberries, whortleberries, and Madeira blueberries. They're easy to tell apart from cranberries and Madeira blueberries—one is red instead of blue, and the other grows in Portugal instead of North America. When it comes to telling blueberries from bilberries, huckleberries, and whortleberries, you have to look inside to spot the difference. While they're all deep blue on the outside, only blueberries have a light green flesh inside. The others are red or purple throughout.

The flowers on blueberry bushes are bell shaped and white, and the blossom end of each berry forms the shape of a perfect five-pointed star. The leaves, which are green throughout the spring and summer, turn lovely shades of crimson and orange during the fall as the temperatures drop.

Blueberry-Apple Crisp

Serves 6 to 8

FILLING

3 cups fresh or frozen blueberries

2 crisp apples, halved, cored, and cut into bite-size pieces

½ cup sugar

3 tablespoons cornstarch

Zest and juice of 1 lemon

¼ teaspoon kosher salt

TOPPING

> 1½ cups all-purpose flour
>
> ½ cup rolled oats
>
> ½ cup sugar
>
> ¾ teaspoon kosher salt
>
> 1 stick (8 tablespoons) unsalted
>   butter, melted

1. Preheat the oven to 375°F.

2. Prepare the filling: Add the blueberries, apples, sugar, cornstarch, lemon zest and juice, and salt to a 2-quart baking dish or a 9-inch square glass pan.

3. Make the topping: In a medium bowl, whisk together the flour, oats, sugar, and salt. Drizzle in the butter while stirring the mixture with a fork until the butter is incorporated and the mixture looks like large and small pebbles. It should hold together when squeezed. Crumble

 Recipe continues

the streusel topping over the fruit, squeezing occasionally to create large and small pieces.

4. Bake for 15 minutes, then reduce the oven temperature to 350°F and continue to bake until the topping is golden brown and the filling bubbles around the edges, 30 to 35 minutes.

5. Remove from the oven and cool at least 10 minutes before serving. Store in the refrigerator for up to 3 days and warm before serving, if desired.

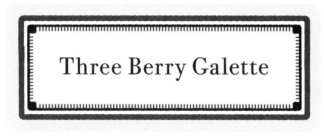

Three Berry Galette

Makes one 9-inch galette

¼ cup cream cheese, at room
temperature

1 large egg, separated

½ cup confectioners' sugar

¼ teaspoon plus 2 pinches of kosher salt

¼ cup granulated sugar

2 tablespoons cornstarch

Juice of 1 lime

1 cup fresh or frozen raspberries

1 cup fresh or frozen blueberries

½ cup roughly chopped strawberries
or blackberries (halved if large)

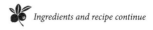

Ingredients and recipe continue

One 12-inch round rolled-out homemade (page 90) or store-bought pie dough

1. Line a sheet pan with parchment paper or a nonstick baking mat and set aside.

2. In a medium bowl, use a hand mixer or rubber spatula to blend together the cream cheese, egg yolk, confectioners' sugar, and a pinch of the salt until smooth and creamy. Set aside.

3. In a large bowl, stir together the granulated sugar, cornstarch, and ¼ teaspoon of salt, then add the lime juice and crumble with your fingers to combine. Add the raspberries, blueberries, and strawberries and toss to coat.

4. Place the pie dough onto the prepared pan. Add the cream cheese mixture to the center and use the back of a spoon to spread it into an even layer, leaving a 2½- to 3-inch border. Mound the berries on top.

5. Fold one side of the dough over the filling, then to its right fold the next bit of dough over the first part, covering the edges of the berries and overlapping and pressing it into the first part to make folded pleats. Continue folding the dough around the rest of the galette. Leave the center 2½- to 3-inch area of the berries uncovered.

6. In a small bowl whisk the egg white with 1 teaspoon of water and the remaining pinch of salt and brush the mixture over the dough. Refrigerate for at least 15 minutes, or up to 2 hours.

7. Preheat the oven to 375°F and adjust an oven rack to the lower-middle position. Bake the galette until the dough is browned and the berries bubble (it's okay if some juice seeps out and around the galette), 50 to 60 minutes. Remove from the oven and cool completely before slicing and serving.

Blueberry-Buttermilk Tartlets

Makes 12 mini tarts

One (17.3-ounce) box puff pastry
   (2 sheets)

All-purpose flour, for rolling

1½ cups buttermilk

½ cup heavy cream

2 teaspoons fresh lemon juice

1 cup sugar

1½ tablespoons cornstarch

¼ teaspoon kosher salt

2 large egg yolks, at room temperature

1 tablespoon unsalted butter

1 to 1¼ cups fresh blueberries

1. Set a 12-cup muffin tin on your work surface.

2. Set the 2 sheets of puff pastry on a lightly floured surface. Use a rolling pin to lightly roll and flatten the sheets of dough until they are slightly thinner than when you began (you're just rolling them slightly). Prick both pieces of dough all over with a fork. Use a 3½-inch cookie or biscuit cutter to press out 12 circles (save the remaining dough for another use if you like). Gently press each circle into a muffin cup (the dough won't reach the top of the cup) and place the tin in the freezer for 30 minutes.

3. Preheat the oven to 375°F. Bake the tart shells until they are light golden brown, 12 to 15 minutes. Remove the pan from the oven and set it on a wire rack—let the shells cool completely in the tin, about 20 minutes.

4. Meanwhile, make the filling: Add the buttermilk, cream, and lemon juice to a medium saucepan. In a small bowl, whisk together the sugar, cornstarch, and salt. Add the sugar mixture to

 Recipe continues

the saucepan along with the egg yolks, whisking well to combine. Cook over medium heat, stirring constantly with a wooden spoon (and making sure to get into the corners of the pan), until a few bubbles pop at the surface and the mixture becomes thick, like a pudding, about 6 minutes. Strain through a fine-mesh sieve and into a large liquid measuring cup, then whisk the butter into the filling.

5. Add about 2 tablespoons of filling to each tart shell and return the muffin tin to the oven. Bake until the filling is dry on top but still jiggles slightly when the pan is shaken, about 15 minutes. Remove the pan from the oven and cool for 30 minutes before removing the tartlets from the pan. Top with the blueberries and serve.

Blueberry Pie

Makes one 9-inch pie

5⅓ cups fresh or frozen blueberries

Zest and juice of 1 lemon

½ cup sugar

¼ to ⅓ cup cornstarch

½ teaspoon plus a pinch of kosher salt

2 disks homemade (page 90) or
   store-bought pie dough

All-purpose flour, for rolling

1 large egg

Vanilla ice cream, for serving
   (optional)

Recipe continues

1. Preheat the oven to 375°F. Adjust one oven rack to the lower-middle position and the other to the lowest position.

2. Add the blueberries to a large bowl and toss with the lemon zest and juice, the sugar, cornstarch (add ¼ cup for a slightly looser filling and ⅓ cup for a tighter filling), and ½ teaspoon of salt.

3. If using homemade pie dough, roll out a disk on a lightly floured surface into a 10- to 11-inch circle. Dust the top of the dough with flour as needed to prevent it from sticking to the pin. Transfer the rolled dough to a 9-inch pie plate, trimming the edges so there is just ½ to 1 inch of overhang, and roll the edges under.

4. Add the blueberries to the pie crust and top with the second rolled-out piece of dough. Trim the edges (if necessary) so there is no more than ½ to ¾ inch of overhang, and then fold the edges under and crimp using your fingers or a fork. Cut a few slits into the top of the dough so the pie vents as it bakes.

5. In a small bowl, use a fork to combine the egg with the pinch of salt and 1 tablespoon of water. Using a pastry brush, coat the top of the pie with egg wash.

6. Set the pie on the lower-middle rack and bake until the top and bottom crust are browned, 55 minutes to 1 hour and 5 minutes. Check occasionally to make sure blueberry juices aren't dripping from the pie—if they are, simply add a foil-lined baking sheet to the lowest rack to catch the drips.

7. Remove the pie from the oven and cool completely before slicing. Serve with ice cream, if desired.

Homemade All-Butter Pie Dough

Makes enough for a double-crust 9-inch pie

2½ cups all-purpose flour, plus
 more for rolling

2 tablespoons sugar

2 teaspoons kosher salt

2 sticks (16 tablespoons) cold
 butter, cut into ½-inch cubes

Ice cubes

1 teaspoon fresh lemon juice or
 apple cider vinegar

1. Add the flour, sugar, and salt to the bowl of a food processor (or to a medium bowl if making by hand). Pulse (or whisk) to combine.

2. Add the cold butter and pulse until the biggest piece is no larger than a small pea, ten to twelve 1-second pulses (or use your fingers or a pastry cutter to blend).

3. Measure 1 cup of water and add a few ice cubes. Add 4 tablespoons of the ice water to the bowl and pulse to combine (or use a fork to mix in). Add 3 more tablespoons of ice water and the lemon juice and pulse until the dough is shaggy and no flour remains in the bottom of the bowl. If it doesn't hold together when you squeeze the dough, add 1 to 2 more tablespoons of ice water and repeat.

4. Turn the dough out onto a lightly floured surface and knead just 2 or 3 times to bring it together, then divide it in half and wrap each in plastic, pressing out into a disk that's about ¾ inch thick. Refrigerate at least 30 minutes, or overnight, before rolling for pie.

No-Bake Blueberry Swirl Cheesecake

Makes one 9-inch cheesecake

½ cup heavy cream

1½ teaspoons unflavored gelatin

¼ cup sugar

8 ounces cream cheese (not whipped),
    at room temperature

Juice of 1 lime

1 teaspoon kosher salt

One 9-inch store-bought graham
    cracker crust

¼ cup homemade (page 10) or
    store-bought blueberry jam

Sweetened whipped cream and fresh blueberries, for serving

1. Add ¼ cup of the cream to a glass measuring cup. Sprinkle the gelatin on top and use a fork to combine. Set aside for 5 minutes to let the gelatin bloom (don't stir), then microwave on high for 30 to 45 seconds, until the mixture bubbles (the gelatin should be completely dissolved).

2. If using a hand mixer, add the remaining ¼ cup of cream to a medium bowl. If using a stand mixer, add the cream to the bowl and fit the mixer with the whisk attachment. Add the sugar to the cream and beat on medium-high speed until the cream holds stiff peaks, 3 to 4 minutes. Add the cream cheese and beat on low until well combined, about 30 seconds. Scrape the bottom and sides of the bowl.

3. Add the lime juice and salt and beat on low to combine, about 30 seconds. Increase the speed

 Recipe continues

to medium-high and beat until well combined and fluffy, 2 to 3 minutes. Add the gelatin mixture and continue to beat for 2 minutes to thoroughly combine. Pour ¼ cup of the filling into a small bowl. Pour the rest into the crust, using a silicone spatula to spread it out evenly.

4. To the mixture in the bowl, add the blueberry jam, stirring until well combined. Add the mixture to a zip-top plastic bag and use scissors to snip off the corner of one end. Squeeze the mixture over the top of the pie—you can use a zigzag motion, you can start in the middle and work in circles outward for a spiral, or you can just squiggle it over the top. Use a long wooden skewer or toothpick to marble the blueberry filling into the plain filling, being careful not to touch the crust.

5. Place the pie in the freezer to set until firm, about 15 minutes (or refrigerate for 2 hours before serving). Serve with a dollop of whipped cream and blueberries.

Blueberry Upside-Down Cake

Makes one 8-inch cake

1¼ sticks (10 tablespoons) unsalted
   butter, melted, plus more for
   the pan

⅓ cup plus ¼ cup packed light
   brown sugar

1 cup fresh or frozen blueberries

Finely grated zest and juice of 1 lime

1½ cups all-purpose flour

½ cup almond meal (almond flour)

2 teaspoons baking powder

½ teaspoon baking soda

½ teaspoon kosher salt

Recipe continues

½ cup milk

Confectioners' sugar, for dusting

1. Preheat the oven to 350°F. Lightly brush the bottom and sides of an 8-inch round cake pan with a little of the melted butter and line with an 8-inch circle of parchment paper. Add 1 tablespoon of the melted butter and spread out evenly across the pan bottom. Sprinkle the bottom of the pan with ¼ cup of the brown sugar, spreading it out evenly. Add the blueberries, distributing them evenly, and sprinkle with the lime zest. Set aside.

2. In a medium bowl, whisk together the flours, baking powder, baking soda, and salt. In a small bowl, whisk together the milk, remaining ⅓ cup of brown sugar, remaining 9 tablespoons of melted butter, and the lime juice. Add the liquid to the flour mixture and stir until combined and no dry streaks remain. Pour the batter over the berries and use a silicone spatula to even it out.

3. Bake until the cake is golden, resists light pressure, and a toothpick inserted into the center comes out clean, 35 to 42 minutes.

4. Remove the pan from the oven and immediately set a plate over the top of the cake. Using oven mitts, carefully hold the cake pan and the plate and flip over the cake so it is centered on the plate. Set the plate down and peel off and discard the parchment circle (rearrange any berries that may come off).

5. Cool completely before dusting with confectioners' sugar and serving.

Blueberry-Coconut Cupcakes

Makes 12 cupcakes

CUPCAKES

Nonstick cooking spray (optional)

2¼ cups cake flour

2 teaspoons baking powder

1½ teaspoons kosher salt

9 tablespoons unsalted butter,
    at room temperature

1¼ cups granulated sugar

2 large eggs plus 1 large egg yolk

¾ cup full-fat coconut milk (whisk
    well before using)

1½ teaspoons vanilla extract

1¼ cups fresh or frozen blueberries

FROSTING

> 6 tablespoons unsalted butter,
>   at room temperature
> 3 tablespoons coconut milk
> 3 cups confectioners' sugar
> Pinch of kosher salt
> 1½ cups sweetened shredded
>   coconut, toasted (optional)

1. Preheat the oven to 350°F.

2. Make the cupcakes: Line a 12-cup muffin tin with paper liners. Spray the tin and liners with nonstick cooking spray, if desired.

3. In a medium bowl, whisk together the cake flour, baking powder, and salt and set aside.

4. Add the butter and granulated sugar to the bowl of a stand mixer fitted with the paddle attachment, or to a large bowl if using a hand mixer. Beat on medium-low speed until

 Recipe continues

combined, then increase the speed to medium-high and beat until light and airy, 2 to 3 minutes.

5. Add the eggs and yolk, one at a time, and beat on medium speed after each addition until the batter is airy, about 1 minute total. Scrape the bottom and sides of the bowl as needed. Stop the mixer and add one-third of the dry ingredients, mixing on low to combine. Add half of the coconut milk and the vanilla and mix on medium-low to combine. Add half of the remaining flour mixture, followed by the remaining coconut milk, and then the last of the flour mixture, mixing after each addition. Scrape the bottom and sides of the bowl to ensure the batter is well combined, then beat on medium-high until light and airy, about 1 minute.

6. Add the blueberries and fold them in, but don't stir too much or the batter will turn blue! Divide the batter among the cupcake liners, filling each nearly to the top, leaving about ⅛ inch of space at the rim. Bake until the tops resist

light pressure and a toothpick inserted into the centers comes out clean, 24 to 26 minutes.

7. Remove the pan from the oven and let cool for 5 minutes, then remove the cupcakes from the pan and cool completely on a wire rack.

8. Once the cupcakes are cool, make the frosting: In a medium bowl with a hand mixer, beat the butter and coconut milk until creamy, 20 seconds. Add 1 cup of the confectioners' sugar and the salt and mix on low until combined. Add the remaining 2 cups of confectioners' sugar, 1 cup at a time, beating on low to combine after each addition and then increasing to medium-high to whip, until the frosting is fluffy, about 1 minute. Use a butter knife or offset spatula to frost each cupcake, and while the frosting is wet, add some coconut to the top of each, if desired. Serve immediately, or store at room temperature overnight. You can also refrigerate the cupcakes for up to 3 days, letting them come to room temperature before serving.

CHANCES ARE YOU DON'T live near a Blueberry Hill (although if you do, lucky you!), but that doesn't mean you can't pick your own blueberries. That might mean going to a u-pick farm that raises highbush berries, but blueberry plants are now easy to grow at home, too, either in the ground or in containers. A bush grown from seed will take two to three years to produce berries, but most nurseries sell young highbush blueberry bushes that are ready to start bearing fruit. For the small and sweet berries that Sal and her mother picked on Blueberry Hill, you'll have to go foraging for lowbush berries or pick them up in the freezer section of your grocery store.

Blueberry-Lemon Pudding Cake

Makes one 9-inch cake

1 tablespoon unsalted butter,
   at room temperature

¾ cup plus 2 tablespoons sugar

¼ cup all-purpose flour

½ teaspoon kosher salt

3 large eggs, separated and at
   room temperature

1 cup milk, at room temperature

Zest and juice of 2 lemons

½ teaspoon cream of tartar

1 cup fresh or frozen blueberries

Recipe continues

1. Preheat the oven to 325°F. Grease a 9-inch
    square glass baking dish with the soft butter and
    set aside.

2. In a medium bowl, whisk together the ¾ cup of
    sugar, the flour, and salt.

3. In a small bowl, beat together the egg yolks,
    milk, lemon zest, and lemon juice. Pour the
    mixture over the flour mixture and whisk until
    well combined.

4. In the bowl of a stand mixer fitted with the
    whisk attachment, or in a large bowl if using

a hand mixer, beat the egg whites on medium speed until foamy, about 30 seconds. Add the cream of tartar, increase the speed to high, and beat until the whites hold stiff peaks, about 1½ minutes. Add the remaining 2 tablespoons of sugar and continue to beat for 30 seconds, until glossy.

5. Add one-fourth of the beaten whites to the batter and gently whisk in to lighten the mixture. Use a silicone spatula to fold in the remaining egg whites.

6. Add about two-thirds of the batter to the greased baking dish, gently spreading it with the rubber spatula. Sprinkle the blueberries over the top. Add the remaining batter in dollops over the berries, gently spreading it out into an even layer as best as you can (it doesn't need to be perfect).

7. Bake until the center is set and resists light pressure, about 35 minutes. Remove the pan from the oven and cool for 10 minutes. Spoon the pudding cake into bowls and serve warm.

Blueberry "Ice Cream"
Bread Pudding

Makes <u>*one 9-inch square*</u> *pan*

2 tablespoons unsalted butter,
   at room temperature

1 pint good-quality vanilla ice
   cream, softened (see Note)

1 large egg

½ teaspoon almond extract

½ teaspoon kosher salt

6 cups 1½- to 2-inch cubes challah
   or brioche bread (½ to ¾ loaf)

1½ cups blueberries

¼ cup sugar

1. Preheat the oven to 350°F. Generously grease a 9-inch square baking pan with the softened butter.

2. Scoop the ice cream out of the container and place it in a microwave-safe bowl. Microwave on high in 20-second bursts, stirring between each, until the ice cream is melted and warm (but not hot). Whisk in the egg, almond extract, and salt.

3. Add the bread to a large bowl and pour the ice-cream mixture over it. Toss to combine.

4. Add half of the bread cubes to the baking pan and sprinkle with about 1 cup of the

Recipe continues

blueberries. Add the remaining bread and top with the remaining blueberries. Sprinkle the sugar evenly over the top.

5. Bake until browned and the center of the bread pudding resists light pressure, 35 to 40 minutes. Remove from the oven and cool at least 15 minutes before serving warm or at room temperature.

~~~~~~ NOTE ~~~~~~

The melted ice cream acts as a custard base. You can substitute a flavored ice cream for the vanilla if you like—varieties such as dulce de leche and ginger are particularly delicious!

Blueberry and Chamomile

Tapioca Pudding

Serves 6

1 cup large pearl tapioca

4 cups whole milk

¼ cup sugar

¾ cup half-and-half

2 chamomile tea bags

1½ cups fresh blueberries

1. Add the tapioca to a large bowl and cover with
    3 inches of cold water. Soak overnight at room
    temperature.

Recipe continues

2. Bring the milk and sugar to a simmer in a large saucepan over medium-high heat. Drain the tapioca and stir it into the milk mixture. Reduce the heat to medium and simmer, stirring often, until the tapioca is tender, 20 to 25 minutes. If the mixture begins to boil, reduce the heat to medium-low.

3. Once the tapioca is tender, set a fine-mesh sieve over a large bowl (you'll be using some of the milk mixture) and drain the tapioca. Pour

the liquid into a container and refrigerate. Transfer the tapioca to the bowl you just used and set aside.

4. Bring the half-and-half to a simmer in a small saucepan over medium-high heat (watch it closely so it doesn't boil over). Turn off the heat and add the chamomile tea bags. Cover the saucepan and steep 5 minutes, then remove the tea bags, squeezing out as much liquid as possible. Discard the tea bags.

5. Pour the chamomile-infused half-and-half over the tapioca and stir to combine, then cover the bowl with plastic wrap and refrigerate until chilled—at least 2 hours, or overnight.

6. To serve: Remove both the reserved milk and the tapioca pudding from the fridge. Add 1 cup of the reserved milk mixture to the tapioca, gently stirring. If you like a looser pudding, add more of the reserved milk mixture. Divide among 6 bowls, top each with ¼ cup of blueberries, and serve.

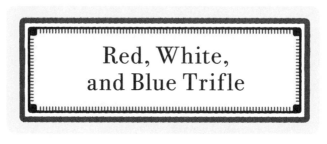

Red, White, and Blue Trifle

Serves 10 to 12

1 pound good-quality white
  chocolate, finely chopped
  (2 to 2½ cups; don't use white
  chocolate chips)
2 cups heavy cream
½ cup plus 3 tablespoons
  granulated sugar
1 teaspoon vanilla extract
Zest and juice of 2 limes
  (3 to 4 tablespoons lime juice)
3½ cups strawberries, hulled and
  quartered

3½ cups fresh blueberries

4 cups crumbled angel food cake
   or pound cake

Confectioners' sugar, for dusting

1. Add the white chocolate to a large heat-safe bowl. To a small saucepan, add 1 cup of the heavy cream and bring it to a simmer over medium-high heat (watch it closely so it doesn't boil over). Pour the hot cream over the chocolate, cover the bowl with plastic wrap, and set aside without stirring for 5 minutes. Remove the plastic wrap and whisk until melted and smooth. Refrigerate the mixture, stirring every 10 minutes, until cooled but not firm, about 30 minutes (this is a great time to hull and quarter the strawberries if you haven't already).

2. While you're stirring and cooling the chocolate mixture, whip the cream: In a large bowl or in the bowl of a stand mixer fitted with the whisk attachment, add the remaining 1 cup of cream

Recipe continues

along with 3 tablespoons of the granulated sugar and the vanilla. Whip using a whisk, a hand mixer, or a stand mixer until the cream is thick and holds stiff peaks. Whisk the whipped cream into the cooled white chocolate mixture and set aside.

3. Add the lime juice to a small saucepan with the remaining ½ cup of granulated sugar and ½ cup of water. Bring to a simmer over medium-high heat, stirring to dissolve the sugar. Once

dissolved, stir in the lime zest. Add 2½ cups of the strawberries and 2½ cups of the blueberries to a medium bowl and pour the lime syrup over the fruit. Stir to coat all the fruit.

4. Add 1⅓ cups of the cake crumbs to the bottom of a 3½- to 4-quart straight-sided trifle dish. Spoon a third of the fruit (and syrup) over the cake. Add a third of the white chocolate whipped cream, using the back of a spoon to even it out. Top the cream with half of the remaining cake, followed by half of the remaining fruit (and syrup) and half of the cream. Repeat with the remaining cake, remaining fruit, and remaining cream.

5. Cover the trifle with plastic wrap and refrigerate for at least 30 minutes (or up to overnight). Top with the remaining 1 cup of strawberries and 1 cup of blueberries, dust with confectioners' sugar, and serve.

Blueberry-Rhubarb Parfaits

Makes 4 parfaits

¼ cup freshly squeezed orange
   juice (from about ½ orange)
½ cup plus 1 tablespoon sugar
1¼ pounds rhubarb, ends trimmed
   and cut crosswise ½ inch thick
Pinch of kosher salt
¾ cup fresh or frozen blueberries
1 cup heavy cream

1. In a medium saucepan, bring the orange juice
    and ¼ cup plus 1 tablespoon sugar to a boil over
    medium heat. Add the rhubarb and salt and
    return to a boil, then reduce the heat to medium-

low and simmer until the rhubarb begins to break down and is nearly tender, about 6 minutes (only stir 2 or 3 times—stirring too much makes the rhubarb mushy).

2. Add the blueberries and continue to cook until the rhubarb is tender and the blueberries are soft (and perhaps have burst), 1 to 2 minutes longer, stirring just once throughout. Transfer to a bowl, cover, and refrigerate until the mixture is well chilled, at least 2 hours, or overnight.

3. Pour the cream into the bowl of a stand mixer fitted with the whisk attachment, or add it to a medium bowl if using a hand mixer. Add the remaining ¼ cup of sugar and beat on low speed until small bubbles form, about 45 seconds. Increase the speed to medium-high and beat until the cream forms soft peaks, about 45 seconds.

4. Spoon about ¼ cup of the rhubarb mixture into each of 4 tall glasses or medium bowls. Top each with ¼ cup of the whipped cream. Repeat, so you have 4 layers with the whipped cream on top. Serve immediately, or refrigerate for up to 2 hours before serving.

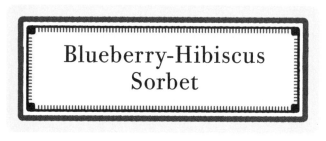

Blueberry-Hibiscus Sorbet

Makes 1 quart

1 cup sugar

4 hibiscus tea bags (such as Red
   Zinger) or other herbal tea bags

4 cups frozen blueberries

¼ cup agave syrup or honey

1. Add the sugar and 1 cup of water to a medium saucepan and bring to a simmer over medium heat. Stir occasionally until the sugar is dissolved, 2 to 3 minutes. Add the hibiscus tea bags, turn off the heat, and steep for 10 minutes.

2. Remove and discard the tea bags and pour the liquid into an airtight container. Refrigerate until well chilled, at least a few hours.

3. Pour the chilled liquid into the jar of a blender and add the blueberries with the agave. Blend until smooth, stopping and using a silicone spatula as necessary to stir the mixture and keep it blending. Pour into a flat-bottomed container (an 8½ × 4-inch inch loaf pan is perfect). Cover with aluminum foil and freeze until firm, at least 2 hours, or overnight. Scoop and serve.

Blueberry Cookies-and-Cream
Milkshake

Makes 2 milkshakes

1 pint vanilla ice cream

1 cup whole milk, plus more if needed

¼ cup homemade (page 10) or store-
   bought blueberry jam
   or ½ cup fresh blueberries

½ cup crushed Golden Oreo Sandwich
   Cookies (chocolate Oreos work,
   too, but your shake will be darker)

1. Add the ice cream, milk, and blueberry jam
    or fresh blueberries to the jar of a blender and
    blend on high until smooth and combined. If
    you prefer a thinner milkshake, add more milk.

2. Add the cookies and pulse to combine. You want
    the cookies to be fine enough to go through a
    straw, but not completely pureed into the shake.

3. Divide between 2 glasses and serve with straws.

Blueberries for Sal was a Caldecott Honor Book in 1949, one of two honors and two medals that Robert McCloskey won for his work as an author and illustrator of children's books. Maine, the setting of *Blueberries for Sal*, was near to McCloskey's heart. He spent summers on a small island off the coast of Maine with his family during his children's childhoods. He and his wife eventually moved to the island full time and he lived there until his death in 2003.

Half of Robert McCloskey's eight picture books are set in Maine: *Blueberries for Sal, One Morning in Maine, Time of Wonder,* and *Burt Dow, Deep-water Man.*

Library of Congress Cataloging-in-Publication Data has been applied for.

ISBN 978-0-593-58040-0
Ebook ISBN 978-0-593-58041-7

Printed in the United States of America

Recipe Developer: Raquel Pelzel
Editor: Deanne Katz
Designer: Danielle Deschenes
Production Editor: Joyce Wong
Production Manager: Kelli Tokos
Copy Editor: Shelley Berg
Marketer: Allison Renzulli

Book and cover design by Danielle Deschenes
Illustrations on pages 10, 12, 21, 27, 30, 33, 47, 57, 74, 88, 97, 106, 109, 110,
116, 122, and 125 by Piers Sanford

10 9 8 7 6 5 4

First Edition